THE POOP ON THE SIDE OF THE ROAD

Written by: Jennie Peach

Illustrated by: Jennie Peach & Kelsey Hawley

Published by Realization Press
in the USA

All Rights Reserved. No part of this publication may be reproduced in any form or by any means, including scanning, photocopying, or otherwise without prior written permission of the copyright holder.

Copyright Jennifer Davis © 2018

DEDICATION

This kooky and silly book is dedicated to my daddy,

Mr. Vaughn Yeomans.

I wanted to pass this unconventional bedtime story on that he used to tell me, so that other kids will get a kick out of it like I did! Mason, his grandson sure does!

Your lighthearted and jovial spirit is missed every single day and your legend lives on!

ACKNOWLEDGMENTS

Drew Becker of Realization Press, Raleigh, NC, thank you for helping me create and write this book with your knowledge and experience.

Sam, my husband, thank you for the support during this process and the belief in its success.

Mason, my son, who with the love for this story, inspired me to make it into a book, thanks sweet boy!

PREFACE

Rusty the Poop is kind of sad on such a happy looking day. He just hangs out by the road feeling lonely, finding it hard to make friends.

One day, things take a crazy turn for Rusty. He realizes he doesn't need to be so sad, but instead has hope, because with the kindness of an unlikely stranger, happiness is on its way!

Rusty, the poop, is sitting on the side of the road one sunny day. He feels very lonely as he watches the cars go by. He feels sad even though it is sunny and cheery outside.

A little gray dog comes walking by and Rusty starts to feel hopeful. Maybe I have found a new friend, thinks Rusty.

As the little gray dog walks up, he lifts his little gray leg and pees on Rusty's head! He then trots away into the distance.

Rusty really feels bad now. He sheds a few tears. The sun starts to go down and he falls asleep.

The next day, Rusty is all dried out from the sun, feeling like a rock. He looks up and sees Spot, another dog, getting closer. Spot is a BIG dog with long legs and a BIG body! Rusty gets really worried!

**Spot gets close and sniffs him.
He notices that Rusty is worried.**

What do you think happens next?

"Not to worry," says Spot, as he wags his tail in a friendly way. Rusty starts to feel a lot better!

Dark clouds start to fill the sky and it begins to rain. Spot quickly digs a hole and says to Rusty, "Get in here to stay dry."

"But the rain will come in the hole and I'll get wet," says Rusty.

"That's OK, I'll protect you," says Spot.

Rusty jumps in the hole. Spot then sits on the hole so no rain gets in.

Half an hour later, the sun starts to come out as the rain stops.

Rusty starts to smell something familiar. He notices right away he is not alone!

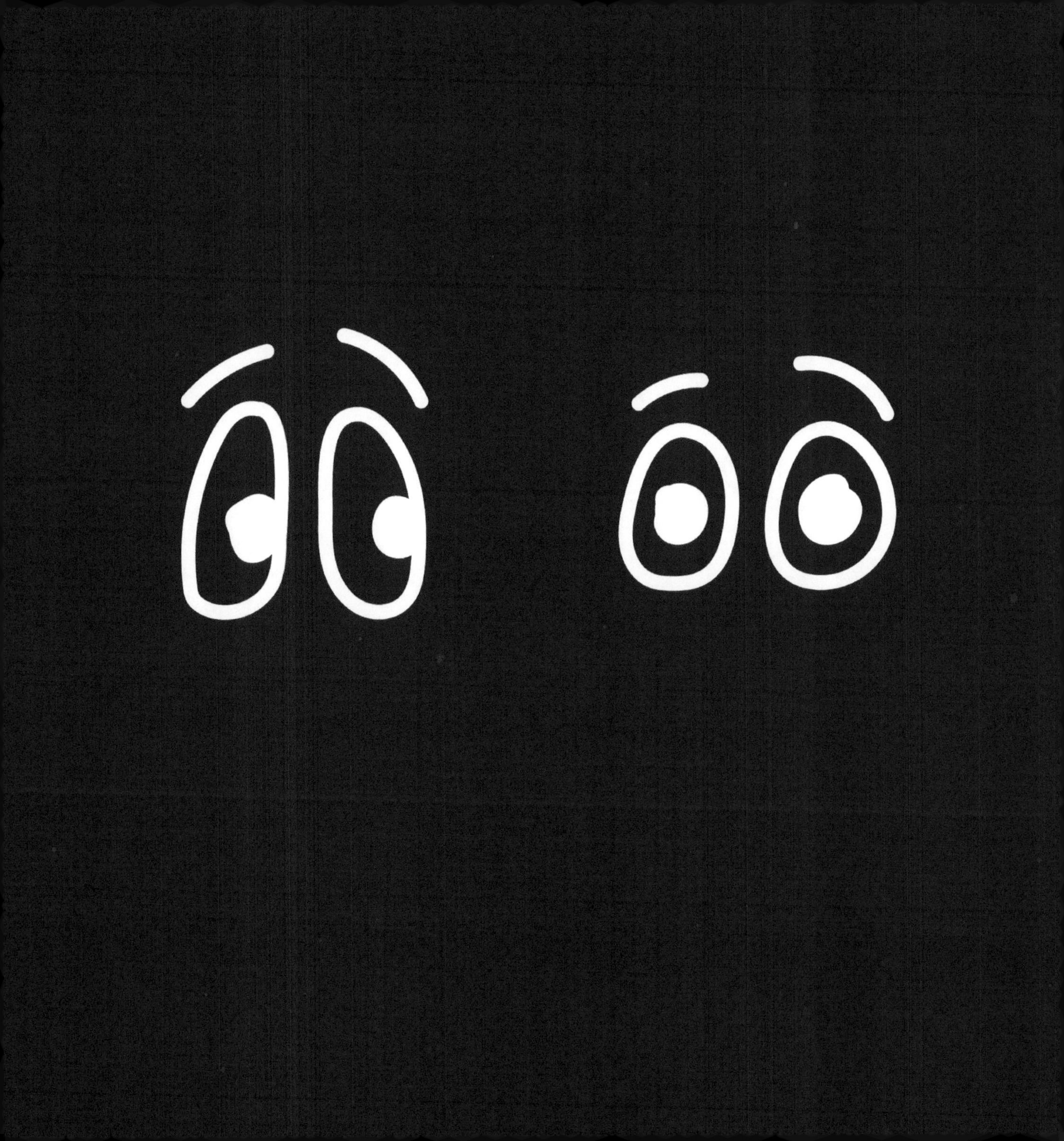

Spot stands up. He's curious as a loud truck rumbles by.

Rusty realizes, Wow! I have a friend that's just like me!

"Thank you so much," says Rusty to Spot. "I had a bad day then you turned it into a great one!"

Spot walks away feeling great because he made someone else feel great!

THE END

www.ingramcontent.com/pod-product-compliance
Lightning Source LLC
Chambersburg PA
CBHW050756110526
44588CB00002B/22